MY LIFE WITH JESUS

GALACTIC GRANDMOTHER PAST LIFE SERIES

APRIL AUTRY

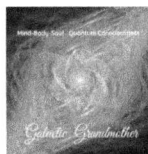

ALSO BY APRIL AUTRY

Galactic Grandmother Past Life Series

ATLANTIS, JOURNEY FROM THE INNER TEMPLE

ESCAPE FROM MALDEK

Galactic Grandmother Spiritual Journey Series

WORKING IN THE QUANTUM FIELD, BOOK 1 & 2

MULTIDIMENSIONAL ASPECTS - HIGHER SELVES

PROLOGUE

In 1981 I took several past life regression classes, during which students took turns lying down on a mat in the center of a darkened room. Two teachers facilitated the regressions, and each student was sent home with a tape recording of their personal regression.

The purpose of these regressions was to observe a past life, which could connect circumstances, lessons, phobias, or people to our current life. After attending these classes, I began to have spontaneous past life regressions, that caught me off guard, yet offered invaluable revelations about my current life.

My Life with Jesus is one of my past life regressions from the guided classes.

CHAPTER 1

*D*ust blew across the barren desert toward me. I pulled up my scarf to cover my nose and mouth, watched strangely dressed men sitting on camels pass by and kick up the sand. I stood guard in front of my tent, where inside my wife and small son still slept. We had stopped along the road to eat and sleep, yet it was dangerous to be the only tent here. There was much activity along the road to Bethlehem, with families, traders and others making their way to the city center to register.

I shifted from one leg to the other and crossed my arms in front of me. I was angry, like many, that we must disrupt our lives and travel to register. I felt I should have the freedom to live my life without being accountable to a foreign army that held dominion over us. It made me feel less of a man, and even though it was Jewish men doing the job of registering, it was the Romans that held us by the throats making demands.

Not only did I have to leave my leather smith shop, I had to put my family in danger traveling. There were reports of men robbing and raping, then disappearing into the desert. I heard my son saying mama and knew he wanted to suckle his mother's breast. I turned and pulled open the heavy fabric of the door, stepped in, and quickly pulled the door closed behind me. I saw my wife and son together under a blanket, and my wife looked up at me with a smile.

"Tea?" I asked her.

She nodded and stroked our son's head, which was cradled in her arm as he drank.

I had heated water for my tea and poured it in her cup with leaves. Steam rose up, and the water turned brown. I sat the cup down near her.

"I'll wait until he is finished." She told me.

I sat down across from her. "Let's try to make it to the oasis."

She nodded.

"I'll feel safer if we sleep near other families." I told her.

"I was told there will be fresh water and dates." She said.

She looked down at our son, and my heart warmed to see the love and care she gave him. I thanked God every day for this beautiful woman, she is a good wife and mother, and I was truly blessed. I watched my wife gently lay our sleepy son down and pick up her tea. She pushed her hair back and took in a deep breath.

"I will be glad to return home." She said.

"Yes," I told her, "carrying Joseph has been harder than you thought."

She nodded and sipped her tea while I admired her. I couldn't think of my life without her, she had been in my life since we were children. We were friends, and as she grew, her beauty made her desired by many young men. I believed that she would marry the son a of a wealthy family, and she could have picked from several, yet she picked me. She came to me after our cousins' wedding and told me that she dreamed we would marry someday. I stood looking at her and could say nothing. She seemed to be a girl destined for a better life than I could give her. She looked at me and tilted her head.

"Would you like this?" She asked.

"I," I hesitated, "I thought you would marry Simon," I said, "he can offer you more than I can."

"No," She said firmly, "I will marry you Samuel."

I nodded, "I would like this."

She smiled, turned and walked away. I watched her go, and she looked back to see me and smiled again. I ran to my parents and told them. My mother clapped her hands and praised God for such a girl picking her son.

"Praise God!" She shouted and walked excitedly to tell her sister.

My father put his hands on my shoulders. "I will speak to her father, then you will begin to work with me. You will learn to work leather so you can care for a family."

My apprenticeship began when I was fourteen, and by the age of sixteen the marriage was arranged and prepared by our parents. Rachel and I were married on a beautiful day in the spring, when the rains had watered the wild grass and the sun made it grow bright and green across the desert. We moved into a small room that was built behind my father's house, and we shared the common areas. Rachel cooked and cleaned in the kitchen with my mother, and I worked with my father in his leather shop. We were happy and soon Rachel's belly swelled with our son. When he was born, both our families and many friends celebrated. We named him Joseph after Rachel's father and Samuel after me.

We took down the tent, I folded it and wrapped it with a leather rope I made, before strapping it and the bedding on my back. Our water pot and cups hung from the rope, my wife carried our son who slept on her back in a cloth, and a small basket with bread, tea, oil and water. We had travelled two days and two nights, and we would need to travel two more days before we reached Bethlehem.

"I am glad you are strong." She told me.

"I am glad that you are strong." I replied and laughed, "Yet I will buy a donkey to go home."

We walked and spoke of many things. We grew up in the same village and our families were joined not only by our marriage, but by our older cousins' marriage. We knew our neighbors so well they seemed extended family. We shared religious holidays, family celebrations and passing of elders. We witnessed marriages and births of children, and when our son was born, he was welcomed with great joy by all. I enjoyed my life in this small remote village, and only traveling men selling fabrics, pots, tea and other goods visited. They often traded or bought leather goods from me. I was happy and rarely angered until the Romans began to make demands.

~

MY THOUGHTS ARE DISTRACTED by a child crying, and I watch the child's mother go to her. She speaks to the child and picks her up. I look out across where I live, and I am grateful for this place I now call home as an old man. I enjoy peace and serenity, and life is orderly. The Essenes strive to follow what they believe God wants. They are kind and accepted me when I needed to heal my heart. Although I never converted to their religion, as they grew to know me, they believed I also followed God's calling to live a pure life, and they respected my work as a scribe. I earned my place here by teaching children to read and write.

I find myself thinking back more and more on my earlier life and wonder if this means that I am getting ready to pass. If my death is coming, I am ready. I have lived a satisfying life, with many happy times, and I feel that I have gained wisdom along the way. When I remember the early times in my life, the love of family, working with my father, and feeling submerged in the blanket of security that life offered, I am glad that I was innocent to the world. I knew nothing of politics then, of how our religious elders in the Temple would retain their power by conspiring with the Romans. I knew nothing of how my personal choices would change the course of my life, and although I do not regret my decisions, they came with great personal sacrifice.

CHAPTER 2

This morning is beautiful, the sky is bright blue with small white clouds, and the air feels good to breath. I have bought leather and carry it over my shoulder as I return to my shop. I walk through the narrow street with vendors on each side. The smell of fresh bread, meat and fish makes me hungry.

"Samuel!" My friend Jacob called out as I pass his shop.

"Jacob!" I stop and call back.

Jacob waves for me to come and reaches out a small loaf of bread to me.

I smile, "This is what I needed!"

Jacob laughed, "Be blessed my friend."

"Will I see you later?" I ask.

Jacob nods, "Yes, I'll be there."

"Good." I take a bite of bread, "Thank you!"

Jacob smiles, and turns to sell bread to a woman.

The bread is delicious, and I have finished it before I reach my shop. I see my father bent over punching holes in a strip of leather.

"Is that the belt for David?" I ask.

"Yes." He answers without looking up.

I walk past him to the room at the back of the shop. I throw the leather down from my shoulder on a table, sort through it and put the pieces on shelves. Although we make all kinds of leather goods, my specialty has become sandals. I improved the comfort of the soles by adding extra leather for padding, I also work the leather for the straps that cover the foot, so it is soft and doesn't rub. After making the first pair of sandals like this for an elder woman, she was so happy that she told all her family and friends. Soon I had stacks of orders, and it has not stopped. I make these comfortable sandals for men, women and children, and also for traders that found they were easy to sell.

The village has grown into a city with many new families. I no longer know all the people that live here, as well as the many traders and others that pass through. We have built a temple for the priests that live here, we have a physician and there are many shops on the street where our leather shop is, including shops for bread, oil, weavers, woodworkers, silversmiths, potters and makers of other needed goods. I have prospered and now live in my own house with Rachel and our three children, Joseph, Rebecca and Ruth.

Joseph is at the age when he should learn a trade, I want him to work with me, yet he has not made a commitment to it. He delivers our leather goods, yet he is not serious like I was at his age. I knew that I must support Rachel and a family, so I prepared for it. Joseph does not know who he will marry, and he seems happy to have his mother care for him. I have spoken to Rachel about this, yet he is her first born and only boy, and she is happy to pamper him until he finds a woman of his own. I shake my head thinking of this.

"He will not grow into a man." I have told Rachel, yet she just smiles.

My girls are beautiful like their mother, and they sit in front of me after dinner, so that I may read the Torah. Living a good life according to our religious teachings is very important to me, and I believe that as their father, I should instruct them to be obedient to God's word. I also did this for Joseph, as well as religious training with the priests, that he attended with boys his age.

My home, my wife, my children and my work have all filled my heart. I am happy and feel satisfied with my life. I share these feelings with my good friend Jacob, and we spend much time together with our wives and children. Today we plan to take our families to listen to the prophet that will speak on the hill outside our village.

I grab sandals that I will finish today and join my father in the shop that faces the street.

"You will see this prophet?" My father asks.

"Yes, Jacob and I will take our families."

"The priests do not like him," my father said, "they say he is defiant."

"I have heard this spoken of him." I say, "yet I will hear him and make my own decision."

~

RACHEL AND SARAH, Jacob's wife, spread blankets out and sat with our children enjoying dates and tea, while Jacob and I stood next to the dirt trail waiting on the prophet. I was interested to know what he would say, while others were ready to condemn him before he spoke a word.

"There!" Jacob said and pointed.

I saw a large group walking up the hill. I kept my eyes on the man leading the group, so that I might see who caused such controversy. As they got closer, the man in front was wearing a white robe with belt and a blue cape that fell down to the ground. He looked much younger than I expected, younger than me, and he was slender. He had light brown hair, a small beard, and a long narrow nose. He looked ahead where he walked until he reached me, then turned his head toward me, and his blue eyes looked deeply into mine. A feeling came from him, he made me feel love such as I felt for my family, and his eyes seemed wise beyond his age. He walked past me before stopping not far away.

"He is young." I heard Jacob say, yet I could not speak.

Yeshua spoke of many things and his words were all I could hear. I did not hear my wife or children, nor any person around me. I was enraptured by what this young man said, and I knew he must truly be a prophet. I felt God speaking directly to my heart through Yeshua, and my eyes filled with tears. I felt such joy and when he finished, I wanted to hear more. Many people gathered closer to him, asking him questions. I wanted to join them, yet I felt a tugging on my sleeve and turned to see Rachel.

"The girls are tired," she said, "we must go."

I looked at my daughters and knew this was so, yet I looked back at Yeshua. I was not ready to leave.

"Samuel." Rachel said, "help me."

She handed me the blanket she had folded and the basket with cups, then grabbed our daughters' hands. She walked past me, and joined Sarah with her children, to walk down the hill. I looked back at the large gathering around Yeshua.

"I liked him." Jacob said.

I looked at him, and remembered he stood by me while the prophet spoke, yet I was unaware of him before.

"Yes," I told him, "I do not know why the priests say he speaks heresy."

"Look at the crowd, more people follow him than go to temple." Jacob said.

It was true, the crowd had grown larger while Yeshua spoke, and now filled the hillside.

"Come," Jacob said, "our wives will be angry if we don't walk with them."

Jacob and I walked quickly to follow our families, yet my thoughts could not leave Yeshua.

CHAPTER 3

"*N*o! No!" I yelled loudly and sat up, shaking. I was in my bed and looked down at Rachel.

"What is it?" She asked.

"Just a dream, go back to sleep." I told her, yet my heart beat hard, and I was afraid.

I watched her pull the blanket up and close her eyes. I reached out and stroked her hair, then laid back down, turning on my side to look out the window. The moon was big, and light shown in on our floor. I closed my eyes and thought about the dream that woke me with terror. I dreamed that I had returned to our village at night after a trip. As I walked down the dark street, I saw an orange glow ahead, then saw it was my house filled with fire and flames. I ran toward it but knew I had lost everything, I knew that Rachel and our children were gone, and I would never have them in my life again. My eyes filled with tears, and I felt the water roll down my face.

I loved my wife and children. I was their protector and provided for all their needs. We had a kitchen filled with food for our family and visitors, Rachel always kept more than we needed and gave food away to others. We had coins hidden in our room, in a secret space in the floor, and I could take days away from the shop without worry. I had worked hard and become successful. I provided Rachel with a comfortable life, and she often reminded me of that.

"I did not need to marry the son of a wealthy man," she would say, "you have given me everything I wanted."

I was happy with my life, yet after I saw Yeshua speak, I could not stop thinking of him. Another day passed and I went to temple, yet the priests said nothing new. I heard all the old passages and knew all the old rituals. I wanted to hear new ideas, new ways of speaking about God such as Yeshua taught. I wanted to learn more from him, and when Jacob said his younger brother was arranging a trip to follow Yeshua, I felt overwhelmed with the feeling that I needed to go.

"You?" Jacob said, "You have a family, and a shop."

I nodded, "Yes, I will ask Rachel to come with me."

Jacob laughed, "She will not travel again! She has said so many times."

He referred to when Rachel and I traveled to Bethlehem.

"Then I will go." I told him.

Jacob took in a big breath and blew it out. He looked down at his feet and shook his head.

"I have a bad feeling about this Samuel."

"Why? I will take a small trip."

Jacob looked up at me, "You will leave Rachel and your children?"
I watched his face closely.

"You have never left them." He said.

I nodded, "This is true, yet I feel called to learn more of God."

"You cannot learn from the priests?" he asked.

"They have taught me all they can." I told him.

"Your shop, haven't you just begun Joseph's training?"

"My father enjoys teaching Joseph and says he will teach him as he taught me."

Jacob kicked his sandal in the dirt and looked me in the eyes. "This is what you want?"

"Yes." I said with conviction, "I feel I must do this."

"I will tell my brother," Jacob said, "and let you tell Rachel."

We both laughed and I put my hands on his shoulders. "Thank you, brother."

~

WHEN I TOLD Rachel that I wanted to go with Jacob's brother, she was not angry with me. I asked Rachel to come with me, yet she was content to stay home. After our trip to Bethlehem, she did not want to travel again. She said that she would be busy sewing new dresses for the girls, and that Joseph could fetch what she needed from the shops.

She smiled, "You are a good man Samuel, and if you learn more about God from Yeshua, our family will be blessed."

I put my arms around her. "Thank you. You bless me."

I did not feel bad about leaving my family, I knew they were safe, and Jacob said he would watch over them while I was gone. I instructed Joseph that he was man of our house while I was away, and I believed this would be good for him. My father said that he would continue teaching Joseph to work with leather.

"You are a good teacher." I told him.

"Is this what I taught you?" My father asked, "That you leave your family, and your shop, to follow a prophet?"

"You are a good father," I said, "you taught me well, yet I must learn more of God."

My father shook his head, "Go to temple!"

~

THOMAS, Jacob's brother, and I walked beside our donkeys. We left home before the sun rose and had ridden the donkeys all morning, stopped for a meal, then started again. The donkeys carried tents, food, water, and other goods. We did not want to over burden the animals, so we decided to walk later in the day when the sun was strongest. We followed the road that Yeshua had taken when he left our city. We did not know when we would see him again, yet traders we met on the road, said he was not far ahead. He stopped in each village, and at each temple to teach. We heard many others had begun to follow him, and that we would find their camps outside the villages.

The freedom of being responsible for only myself was a new adventure. I had lived at home answering to my parents, then married and built my life with Rachel and our children. Traveling alone was exciting, and Thomas was a good guide. He had not married, choosing to explore many exotic places that he told me about. We also discussed Yeshua's teachings on the hillside, and I knew with each step, I was closer to hearing Yeshua speak again.

Thomas led us along the road which slowly went down toward the vast stretch of water on our right. Suddenly he stopped.

"I see a city," he said and pointed down, "and it looks like many tents outside the city."

I walked with my donkey to stand beside him and looked where he pointed.

"Yes!" I said excitedly. "That must be where Yeshua's followers are camped!"

"Praise God!" He shouted.

We were excited to be this close to joining Yeshua and walked quickly toward our destination.

~

"WILL YOU JOIN US?"

I looked up from the parchment I wrote on.

"I am sorry, what did you say?" I asked.

"Will you join us for the evening meal." Alexsandra asked again.

I nodded and smiled. "Thank you, it would be my honor."

The young girl smiled and ran back toward her home. I watched her go and looked around the village. Men had returned from fishing, women collected clothes that had dried in the sun, and the elders, including me, sat in the shade. While the grandmothers and grandfathers gathered in separate groups, with women sewing and men discussing today's fishing catch, I sat alone at a wooden table. I was often asked to join a family for the evening meal, many people here called me uncle. I was a trusted member of my community and had grown into the role of an elder and teacher.

Since I have been thinking much about my younger life, I have started to write about it. Not just about my life, but also of Yeshua and his teachings. I want to record his words, and his work as accurately as possible. Although I was not a disciple, I did become devoted to Yeshua. I made sandals for him and others and helped in any way I could. I was always close by when he taught, as his words were sweet as honey to me. After he was killed my heart broke for the first time, and I grieved his passing for many years.

When I remember being younger, what I did and what I looked like, it seems I am watching someone else. The younger Samuel lived in another time, he felt differently than I do now, and he made decisions that were both brave and naïve. I am glad that I did not know what was to come, because I lived each moment with enthusiasm. I do not regret when I followed Yeshua, because those were magical years, I saw him do things that made me believe in the impossible.

"God moves through us," he said, "as I love you, so does God."

CHAPTER 4

My heart pounded with excitement as we walked through the streets of this busy city, Thomas stopped to buy fresh bread, and handed me the rope to his donkey. I waited impatiently. I wanted only to see Yeshua, and to know when he would speak again. Thomas took a big bite of bread and smiled.

"You're not hungry?" He asked.

"Rachel packed many loaves in my bag." I replied.

"I would have such a wife as yours." Thomas said and smiled.

"I am blessed." I told him.

I handed him the rope and looked around. "Let's go to his encampment."

Thomas nodded and we walked down the street past the shops, and past houses until we saw the tents. They had formed their own small village with tents. There were tents on each side of a path, and the path ended by circling around a larger tent. A carpet was laid outside the door of this tent.

"This must be Yeshua's." I said.

Thomas stopped and we looked around. "Where should we put our tents?"

Tents were also behind Yeshua's tent, so I pointed further back where there was enough room for our tents and donkeys. "There."

After we set up our tents, fed and watered our animals, we looked back toward Yeshua's tent. The sun was lower in the sky, and people were starting small fires for tea and food. I wondered where Yeshua was and kept watch on his tent.

"Do you think he will speak tonight?" I asked Thomas.

"I hope he does," Thomas answered, "we have traveled far to hear him."

~

YESHUA DID SPEAK THIS NIGHT. He returned from the city, followed by many, and stood on the carpet before his tent. Women put candles around the carpet so that we might see him more clearly, and the light flickered upon Yeshua as he spoke. I sat on the dirt with the others and dove into his words as if diving into water. My eyes filled with tears many times, and many times my heart opened with the love that came from Yeshua. Then he raised his hand signaling he had finished, and I heard a sigh come from his followers, as it did from my own mouth. I had not eaten any food this evening, yet what he said of God filled me.

We watched Yeshua go into his tent, then we walked to ours. I looked up at the night sky, wondering if God looked down upon us.

"I have never heard priests speak like this." I said.

"He does not read from a book, nor say the old passages." Thomas replied.

"He teaches us new ways," I said, "I feel I know more of God."

Thomas nodded. "Yes."

We said goodnight and went into our tents. I rolled my blanket out and found a flower, I knew that Rachel put it there and I smiled. I lay down and breathed in deeply to smell its fragrance. It reminded me of Rachel, and I wished she was here with me, yet I understood her feelings. She enjoyed our home, and it was easier to care for our daughters there. I told her that my trip would last a month, then I would return. Yet I had not known then, how Yeshua's teachings would compel me to travel on, to learn more and satisfy something deep within me.

I awoke to the sounds of people. I stretched my arms out and crawled from my tent. People were taking down their tents, and I saw that Yeshua's tent was already packed upon a donkey. I did not see Yeshua.

"Thomas!" I called out.

I heard Thomas moving in his tent, then his head appeared out the door.

"What is it?" He asked.

"People are taking their tents down," I told him, "Yeshua will be leaving."

Thomas climbed out of his tent and scratched his beard. "I need to buy more bread before we leave."

We took our tents down, packed them on our donkeys and started for the village. While Thomas bought bread, I waited and looked around to see Yeshua or his followers. As he loaded his bread into a bag, I saw a group of people approaching from a side street.

"There." I pointed for Thomas to see.

They came closer, and we heard them talking excitedly, praising God and Yeshua.

"What is this?" Thomas asked a man.

"Yeshua healed the servant of a Roman!" The man answered as he passed.

The noisy crowd continued to walk past us, and Thomas looked at me. "He healed a servant?"

I looked for Yeshua and did not see him.

"Let's go back to the encampment and wait for Yeshua with the others." I told Thomas.

While we waited, we heard more stories about what Yeshua had done. Thomas and I were astounded at what we heard.

"Could this be true?" Thomas asked me.

I shook my head, "I do not know."

Yeshua returned when the sun was high above us, he drank tea offered to him by a woman, and smiled at us waiting around.

"Will you tell us how you healed the servant?" A man asked.

"I will say only this, "Have faith in God," Yeshua smiled, "Know our Father will heal you."

"You healed the servant!" The man said.

"God healed him," Yeshua told him firmly, "give praise to God."

Yeshua finished his tea, and when he returned the cup, he said thank you to the woman so sweetly as if he blessed her.

~

THOMAS AND I, the disciples and followers left the encampment to follow Yeshua through the city. I did not know where we were going, yet I felt the excitement around me. People had lively conversations, as they led donkeys carrying baskets of supplies. People were curious to see what miracle Yeshua would perform next. I initially followed Yeshua for his teachings, yet now, I also wanted to see him perform a miraculous deed. I did not have long to wait.

We had traveled for two days and came to another city. We were a large crowd that walked behind Yeshua through the narrow streets. We walked by houses and shops, and the local people stood aside watching us. The people in front of Thomas and I stopped. We stood and I heard wailing ahead.

"A funeral." I heard someone say.

I tried to see through the crowd, yet could only see Yeshua's followers. We waited. I knew the funeral procession must be passing. Thomas used his scarf to wipe his face.

"It is hot." Thomas said.

I reached for the water bag that hung from my donkey and took a large drink. It would be good to stop for food and rest. Suddenly I heard a woman scream. I looked at Thomas, and we heard more people crying out. I climbed on my donkey to see over the people's heads and saw Yeshua standing far away with the funeral procession. People were yelling and screaming.

"Do you see anything?" Thomas asked.

"Only Yeshua at the funeral procession." I told him.

"Is there danger? Is he in danger?" Thomas cried out.

I jumped down from my donkey and began to push my way to the front of the crowd. As I got closer to Yeshua, women were crying, and men shouted out. I was blocked from going further and stretched up to see.

"What happened?" I asked to anyone that would answer.

"Yeshua gave life to that woman's son!" Someone said.

I didn't understand what that meant. "He gave life to someone?"

"He brought that dead man back to life." Another person told me.

"How could that be?" I asked.

"I saw it!" A woman told me, "Yeshua walked to the coffin and spoke to the dead man."

"He came back to life?" I asked her.

The woman nodded, with tears covering her face, "He got out of the coffin and went to his mother."

My mouth fell open. "How could this be?" I thought

I stretched again to see ahead, yet the crowd was tightly packed together, so I turned and went back to Thomas. I told him what I heard.

"No!" He shook his head, "this cannot be."

That evening Yeshua retreated with his disciples to a house in the city. Yeshua's followers went outside the city to put up their tents, make fires and talk of what happened that day. Thomas and I heard people tell the story over and over. People that witnessed the miracle cried when they spoke of it. They all told the same story, with the same words that Yeshua spoke. We agreed there was a miracle this day, even if we hadn't seen it.

"I understand why so many follow Yeshua." I said.

"Yes." Thomas agreed, "He truly is a prophet of God."

~

Thomas and I became devoted followers, hoping to see a miracle and feeling blessed each time we heard Yeshua speak. When Yeshua's disciples packed to leave, we did also. Thomas and I traveled far from home, yet we did not speak of it. More than a month had passed when Yeshua left in a boat to speak in another city. He told us he would return, so his followers set up tents by the sea. After a week, Thomas was tired of waiting.

"I am ready to go home." Thomas said.

"He will return." I told him, "and we will hear about his travels, and what he has done."

We waited another week, and as I squatted before our fire making tea, Thomas paced back and forth.

"I am tired of waiting." He said, "We cannot keep following Yeshua."

I watched him, and knew he was frustrated.

"I am tired of this!" Thomas looked at me. "we need to return home, we have been gone too long."

I knew that when Thomas left for home, he would expect me to come with him. I had not slept at night thinking about this. We had been gone longer than we expected, and the journey home would be just as long. I knew that Rachel would wonder why I had not returned, yet I was not ready to stop following Yeshua.

I had gotten closer to Yeshua. I made him a new pair of sandals, the comfortable kind that people enjoyed, and he asked me to make his disciples sandals also. I saw him relaxing with his disciples and saw how he liked to make them laugh. He enjoyed conversations with these men, and also with the women close to him. I saw him as a man now, not only as a prophet. He enjoyed his followers and counseled many privately. He did not want to be treated the same way as the priests. He wanted people to ask him questions, and I asked questions about God when I sewed sandals near him. He was glad to answer, to discuss this with me, and encouraged me to listen to my heart. Mostly, he wanted his followers to love God and each other, and his unselfish ways made us love him.

I prayed for answers about returning home. Was I a bad husband and father if I stayed away longer? Would Rachel think that I abandoned her? Should I ask Yeshua for advice, yet I hesitated. What if he told me to return home? In my heart, I knew I could not, not yet.

"Did you hear me?" Thomas asked, and looked at me.

I nodded and took a deep breath.

"We will leave in the morning." He said.

I looked at him and shook my head. "I cannot."

Thomas pinched his eyebrows together. "You cannot! Why?"

"I am not ready," I said, "I need to learn more."

Thomas crossed his arms across his chest. "When Yeshua returns, he may travel further from our home, and we have already been gone longer than we planned."

"I know this." I said.

"What of your family?" He asked.

I looked into his eyes and hoped he would understand.

"Each time Yeshua speaks, my heart fills with God's love. I am learning more about God from Yeshua, than I ever did from the priests."

"Is this more important than your family?" Thomas asked.

"No, yet I will be a better husband and father when I return." I answered.

"When will you return?" He asked.

"I do not know."

Thomas shook his head, "I will leave in the morning."

"Please tell Rachel that I love her and the children."

"I will tell her yet think on this Samuel. If you are gone too long, you will be abandoning them, and she could take another husband."

"Oh no! I would never abandon them!" I protested, "And Rachel would not take another husband!"

"Yeshua is not a priest," Thomas said, "he has been called a heretic, and if you follow him, you could also be called a heretic."

"You know this is not true!" I protested.

"If you abandon your family, and you are a heretic, Rachel can remarry."

My mouth fell open, how could he say this? I love Rachel.

"She told me to go." I told him, "She knows I would not abandon her."

Thomas shrugged, and began drinking his tea. The sun had gone down and the sky was still lit over the water. I would follow Yeshua a little longer.

"Tell her I will be gone another month." I said.

Thomas looked at me with disgust, then back at the fire and did not speak.

"I love my family." I told him.

The morning sky was grey and cloudy. A cold wind blew across the water against my tent.

"I am glad to leave." Thomas told me and pulled his scarf up to cover his head.

He looked down at me from where he sat on his donkey and shook his head.

"You should return." He told me.

"I will soon." I answered.

He gave a gentle kick to the side of his donkey and rode away. I watched him and a small part of me thought that I should be leaving with him. Yet a larger part was glad to stay with Yeshua longer.

"Rachel will understand." I told myself, then called out to Thomas, "Go with God."

~

I sat in the shade remembering that decision I made. I had not known then how it would change the course of my life. A breeze blew, and I held the parchment down to my writing table. I looked at my hand, now old. I saw blood vessels running under my thin skin and saw that my fingers now looked frail with bony knuckles. I remembered how strong I once was, and how these same hands had worked hard, and also held the hand of the woman I loved. The breeze stopped and I leaned back in my chair. I closed my eyes, and my thoughts drifted back to when Thomas left, and how Yeshua returned the following day.

A loud noise startled me. I opened my eyes and realized that I had been sleeping. I was like the other old men sitting in their chairs and sleeping under the trees during the day. I laughed at myself. When the day is warm with a cool breeze, the comfort of sitting in the shade, becomes an old man's pleasure.

CHAPTER 5

"*H*e is back!" I heard a woman cry out.

"He has returned!" A man yelled happily.

I had been sitting, sewing leather for a bag when I heard the news. I put the bag down and stood up to look across the sea. There is was, a boat came toward us. There were clouds and much wind blowing across the water, and I worried about this when I saw waves hitting the sides of the boat, yet the boat made its way safely ashore. I put the leather in my tent and walked down to see Yeshua.

My days and my nights had become like those of the other followers. We watched and waited for Yeshua, always hoping to see him perform a miracle or hear him speak. I memorized all Yeshua said, by repeating it to myself, and thinking about the meaning of his words. I prayed to become closer to God, and I prayed for my family, yet they seemed to fall away from my daily life. I stopped counting the days that I was gone, and after the first large moon passed, I knew I had broken my promise of returning to Rachel in a month.

"She will understand." I told myself.

Following Yeshua was a life that I embraced. I saw new places and people. I had new friends and we formed a community of believers. We tried to live as Yeshua instructed, we helped each other through the hardships of travel, and we knew that these times were special. We had robust discussions about religion, about Yeshua's teachings, and I was content. At night, alone in my tent, I wondered how Joseph was learning to work leather from my father, and I wondered how Rachel and the girls were doing, yet I knew they were comfortable and safe.

"When I return, I will have many stories to tell!" I told myself.

I did have many stories to tell. I witnessed miracles with my own eyes, I saw Yeshua speak words that healed, that gave life to the dead, and I saw him do what no other man could do. I believed that Yeshua was the prophesied Messiah, and God worked through him. He was both powerful and gentle at the same time. I saw him angry. I felt his anger with priests and their greedy politics, and it dropped me to my knees with fear. I knew if he could give life to the dead, he could also take it away, yet he said only God had the right to do so. His gentle nature, love of people and all else that lived, seemed to be that of an angel. I felt blessed to be in his presence, and I stayed close, hoping for a smile or a chance to speak with him. His other followers felt as I did, and many times Yeshua retreated to a secluded place, so that he could pray and be alone with God.

~

I ROLLED up my parchment and pushed back my chair so that I might stand. My bones were stiff, and as I stepped away from the table, I walked slowly at first. The sun had gone down behind the hills, and there was a glow that came from it, covering the village with beautiful light. I looked forward to my meal, and an interesting conversation. The girl's father, James, was well versed in their religion and enjoyed debating the differences in our beliefs. While I believed that their religion kept them on a good path, I also felt their religion did not offer the freedom of thought that Yeshua taught. Yeshua told his followers that God was both within and without. That seeking answers through prayer and listening to your inner voice were important. He had taught us that priests do not always speak the will of God, nor do they always do what they preach.

~

THE DINNER WAS DELICIOUS, and the conversation was as I expected. We covered a variety of topics and I enjoyed this young family, often wondering what my own children's families would be like. I would be a grandfather, and I missed seeing the children of my children. This family was wonderful, yet no substitute for looking into the eyes of my children and watching them grow older and become parents.

"Samuel."

I looked up from my cup of tea and smiled. "Did I wander from your delightful company?"

The mother, Deborah, put her hand on my shoulder, "Are you finished eating?" She asked.

My plate was empty and wiped clean by bread. I laughed, "I am!"

She took my plate and her daughter, Alexsandra, picked up a bowl with oil and followed her mother away from the table.

"Thank you." I told James, "You treat me like I am family."

"We honor our elders." He said simply, then looked at me with concern.

"You never speak of having a family Samuel," he said, "did you marry?"

I sighed and nodded. "I did."

"You had children?" He asked.

"Yes, I had a son and two daughters."

James looked past me to his wife. She had stopped walking toward us and stood silently. She grabbed Alexsandra's hand and they left the room.

James looked back at me, "Will you tell me of your family?"

I lived here for over thirty years, and never answered questions about my family. These kind people asked about my past, yet never insisted that I speak of it. They accepted me as a man seeking God, a man that arrived in their village alone, with a heart that needed to heal. I heard people speak of me and say that my family must have perished in a tragedy. There was some truth in this, I lost my family which was a personal tragedy, yet one of my own making. I had not wanted to speak of my past, yet now as an old man I was ready.

I looked at James. "It is time that I spoke of my family, and I am happy to share my story with you."

I looked at the candle that sat on the center of the table. It had not burned long, and still stood tall in the bowl that collected the wax.

"Let me start by telling you about how the most beautiful young girl in a small village picked me to be her husband."

James smiled, "I want to hear this."

~

I TOLD James of my early life, my mother and father, and my family. I told him of life in my small village, and how it was during the celebration for my cousin's wedding, that Rachel came to me and said she dreamed we would marry.

James nodded. "God speaks through women also."

I continued with our marriage, and how we happily settled into our new life together. I spoke of our first born, Joseph, and how Rebecca and Ruth followed.

"You were blessed." James said.

"Yes." I agreed., "I was happy. I had a family, a shop with my father, my own home and the life that I always wanted."

"You had a shop?" James asked.

I told him how my father taught me to be a leather smith, and how I made comfortable sandals that many wanted. That our leather business grew with the village, and that I was able to give Rachel and my family a good living.

"You were a leather smith!" He said, "Yet you do not make sandals now."

I laughed, "No, we have a good sandal maker here."

"I do not understand Samuel," James said, "what happened that brought you here alone, and that made you stay?"

I put my hands together as if to pray, then interlaced my fingers, and looked at him.

"Am I ready to speak of this?" I thought.

James watched me and spoke, "You do not have to tell me. I see this causes you pain."

I nodded, "It does, yet I will tell you. I am old, and my story is a lesson that can be used to teach. My story is what happens when God calls you. My story is about renunciation, yet the pain was too great to harvest the wisdom, until I became old."

James mouth fell open, and his eyes never left mine.

I continued, "I was happy with all this world can offer. I had a beautiful wife that was a loving wife and mother. I had children that bless every father. I had a shop and many people that bought leather goods from me, even traders came to buy the comfortable sandals I made, because they could sell them for a profit. I had a good friend, Jacob, that was like a brother to me. Jacob and I enjoyed spending time together with our families. I was grateful for the blessings in my life. I also loved God and was faithful to the priests that guided us."

James nodded, "This is good."

"There was news of a prophet that would speak near my village, so Jacob and I took our families to hear this prophet. His name was Yeshua."

"I have heard many stories about him." James said.

"Yeshua was not liked by the priests, they said he preached against the temple doctrines. I wanted to hear what Yeshua said and make my own decision about this."

"I understand." James told me, "You are a fair man."

"Jacob and I both agreed that Yeshua did not speak against temple doctrines, and Jacob believed the priests were threatened by this new prophet, because he had more followers than those that went to temple."

"Why was this?" James asked.

"I can only tell you how I felt when Yeshua spoke."

I looked at him and thought back to the first time I heard Yeshua on the hill by my village.

"He was full of love. His words were like keys that opened my heart, and tears came to my eyes because I was so filled with the love of God."

James listened quietly.

"Do you remember when Alexsandra was born?" I asked him, "Your heart was so full of love that you may have cried with happiness."

James smiled, "I remember that day. I remember the love I felt for her, and for Deborah."

"When Yeshua spoke, I felt this love. He was young yet he truly was a prophet of God." I told James.

Deborah and Alexsandra walked back into the room.

"We will say goodnight. Thank you for coming to dinner." Deborah said.

"Thank you," I told her, "your food is always delicious."

Deborah and Alexsandra left us, and I looked at James. "I should leave."

"No, please," he said, "we have time. Please finish your story."

I was quiet for a moment, trying to remember how I felt after Yeshua left our city.

"After I heard Yeshua speak, I could not stop thinking about what he said. I felt closer to God after just one teaching from Yeshua, than I had during my whole life from the priests."

"Why was this?" James asked.

"Yeshua spoke from his heart. He did not read from books or sing old scriptures. His words brought God to life, and more importantly, his words made God come alive in me."

"I would like to have heard him." James said.

"My life changed after I heard Yeshua speak. I could not stop thinking about him. I thought of what he said when I was home, and when I was working. I listened to the priests at temple, and their words were now dead to me. I wanted to hear more of Yeshua's teachings, and it was more than just wanting, it was a calling. God was pushing me to leave my life and follow Yeshua so that I could learn more."

"You left your family?" James asked quietly, as if he heard me wrong.

"Yes, I left with my wife's blessings. I traveled with Jacob's brother, Thomas, to follow Yeshua. We only planned to be away a month, yet after what we witnessed, we did not return so quickly."

"What did you witness that would keep you from your family?"

I told him of seeing God work through Yeshua and heal people.

"Oh." James said.

"I also saw him give life back to a man that had died."

James jerked his head back, "How can this be?"

"God worked through him, and I believed him to be the prophesied Messiah."

James nodded, "You witnessed this?"

"Yes James, with my own eyes. I saw miracles that only God could do, and Yeshua did not want praise for it. He always gave praise to God."

"He was humble." James said.

"Yeshua was unselfish and loved all people. He preached that we should love each other as family, and we tried, yet it was our love for him that made us follow."

"How long did you and your friend follow him?" James asked.

"We were gone more than a month, and it would take that long to return to our city when Thomas said he was ready to leave. I had not slept for many nights because I knew Thomas would expect me to return with him, yet I could not."

"You could not?" James leaned forward and placed his elbows on the table, cupping his face with his hands.

"I believed that after I told my wife about Yeshua, that she would understand why I was gone longer than expected. She and my children had food and money, they were surrounded by family and friends, and they were safe. They did not need me to work so they could eat. It is hard for others to understand that I could not return to my family at this time. It is hard for others to know how powerful God is, when he has plans for your life."

"Did God have plans for your life Samuel?"

"He did, although I did not understand that then. I only knew that I could not return home with Thomas. Thomas warned me that Yeshua was being called a heretic, that Rachel could remarry if I followed a heretic, and if she felt that I had abandoned her."

James nodded. "I am aware of this."

"I protested when Thomas said this, I loved Rachel and would never abandon her. I also knew that Rachel loved me, and I believed that she would never divorce me to marry another."

James leaned back, "She thought that you abandoned her!"

I nodded. "I do not condemn her. I understand why she did what she did, and it has not changed my love for her."

"What did she do Samuel?"

I looked at the candle which had burned down half its height, and then to James.

"It is late, and my story is long. It is best that I finish on another day."

"Oh!" James said disappointed, "You must promise to come back soon!"

"I promise." I said, "Will you make a promise to me?"

"Yes." He told me.

"Please do not tell anyone my story, until after I come back and tell you all of it."

"I promise Samuel."

"Thank you, James."

I pushed my chair back and stood. "Thank you for dinner."

"You will be invited back soon!" He said and smiled.

He walked me to the door and watched as left. I turned to wave at him, and I felt good. I am wise enough now, after spending years reviewing what happened, to know that I should not feel guilty for leaving my family and spending precious time with Yeshua. When one receives a Divine calling, there is no personal choice, the Divine calling is always stronger. The pain in my heart had healed many years ago, and I had learned to live a life that I never expected to live. I no longer have a reason not to tell my story, and James is the person I want to tell. I feel certain that he will not judge me, yet if he does, it matters not to me. I am at peace with the outcome of my life.

I lay in bed and felt the breeze gently touch my face. I always enjoyed sleeping next to an open window, I liked the fresh air and I liked to look up at the sky. The sky was very clear, filled with stars that twinkled. Tonight, the moon was just a slice of light, so the stars shone more brightly than usual.

"Thank you for this beautiful night," I prayed, "thank you for the many blessings that I've received during my life. I pray that all those I love, may be filled with faith and hope, and never believe that they are alone."

I closed my eyes and listened to my breath going in and out, and I wondered if dying would be as easy as drifting off to sleep. I am ready to explore what will happen when I step into my next life. Will I see Yeshua again? I look forward to finding out.

CHAPTER 6

"Samuel!" "Samuel!"

I was being called to help someone pull down a tent before the wind did. A storm was blowing in. The sky had big dark clouds full of water, ready to pour down, and the wind was blowing this storm straight toward us. The camp was packing to leave, Yeshua was ready to travel.

I grabbed the tent and helped two other men fold it together, then it was strapped to a donkey's back. I was ready to go, my donkey carried my belongings, and I looked forward to seeing where Yeshua would take us next. I did not know that the storm blowing over us now, would be foretelling the next year and a half of my life. The harsh conditions that suddenly sprang upon us, the disillusionments of witnessing the cruelty of men, and feeling my heart break apart not once but twice. There was a time when I couldn't see a future worth living, yet God guided me, and I found my way to healing.

When we started to travel the wind was at our back, blowing hard with sprinkles of water, then the storm overtook us with water pouring from the clouds. My clothes were soaked, the scarf on my head dripped water into my eyes, and I shook from the cold. I looked ahead and saw no place to shelter, so I followed the rest, as we slowly made our way across the barren landscape. We traveled under the storm all afternoon until it blew past us, then we stopped to make camp and fires.

I squatted next to a small fire and rubbed my hands together. The fire warmed my hands, yet I still wore wet clothes that chilled my bones.

"Would you like some?" A woman asked and offered me a bowl of hot grains.

"Yes, thank you."

I gratefully ate and returned the bowl to the woman. She often fed me, along with her family, and I bought supplies for her when we passed through villages or cities. I knew that I must take off my wet clothes, so I put up my tent and crawled inside. I hung my clothes inside along the side of the tent, and quickly crawled into my blanket. I still shook, yet could feel my body beginning to warm, and I went to sleep.

The next morning my clothes were still wet, and felt cold when I put them on. I left my tent to stand next to a neighbor's fire.

"That was a bad storm!" A man said as he joined us.

I saw his damp clothes hung from his body like mine, and nodded. "Yes, yes it was." I replied.

$\sim$

THAT WAS a storm I would remember. It marked the beginning of events, that took me into a future I could never have imagined possible. By hearing the words of Yeshua, my own inner knowing of God was alive, and by seeing Yeshua embody God's qualities of compassion, love, and Divine wisdom, I believed that he was the Messiah the priests spoke of.

"Surely," I thought, "Yeshua will be praised by the priests, and welcomed by the people."

Yeshua was a bringer of goodness and miracles. His followers grew in numbers, and we were happy being together as a family following Yeshua. Unbeknownst to me, there were sinister circumstances that would prevent the outcome I believed possible.

Looking back now, I believe Yeshua knew the possibilities of what would happen. Perhaps he hoped for the best, yet understood human nature at its worst. Yeshua never faltered in his mission nor changed his teachings to avoid danger. He did leave camp with his disciples many times, and he had the opportunity to escape to safe regions, yet he returned.

"Why does he keep putting himself at risk?" I asked myself, and debated with followers around the fire. We worried when we saw the battles between the priests and Yeshua, if he left us to seek asylum elsewhere, we would have understood.

～

JAMES INVITED ME TO DINNER, and afterwards we sat outside, enjoying the evening and a cup of tea.

"Where did I stop my story?" I asked him.

"Your wife thought you abandoned her." James said.

I nodded, "I understand why she thought this," I told him, "I was gone a year and a half."

James' eyes opened wide. "That is a long time."

"Yes," I said, "and I was following Yeshua, who was a condemned heretic."

James sighed, "Why did you not return to your wife, after the priests condemned Yeshua?"

I looked James in the eyes, "The priests were wrong, Yeshua was the Messiah that was prophesied."

"You believe this?" He asked.

"I saw Yeshua do what no mortal man can do!" I told him.

"Was he a magician or sorcerer?" James asked.

I laughed, "No, he was truly a man of God. He loved God and called him Father."

James shook his head, trying to understand.

"I stayed with Yeshua until I saw him crucified." I told him.

"I have heard about that." James said.

"I later heard that he came back from the dead to see his disciples." I told him.

"Do you believe this?" James asked and watched me closely.

"I saw Yeshua give life to a man already dead in his tomb, then why could he not do the same?"

James shook his head, "I do not understand why the priests condemned Yeshua."

I nodded, "They did not want to give power over to him."

"They would deny God to stay in power?" He asked.

"They did." I said, and felt water come into my eyes when I thought of how Yeshua suffered.

James saw this and grabbed my shoulder. "This must have been terrible to witness."

I nodded. "My heart had been filled with the love of God, Yeshua did that for me. He taught us to love all men, yet I could not love the priests or the Romans that killed him."

"I understand." James told me.

"I did not hate, yet anger filled me, and pain such as I had never felt."

"What did you do?" James asked.

"I started my journey home, and along the way I grieved for Yeshua, yet it helped me to think that I would rejoin my family."

"Oh," James said, "How did your wife greet you when you returned?"

I clasped my hands together and looked down. I remembered the evening when I rode into my city, down the streets that now looked different to me. I passed my shop, which was closed for the night, and listened to families inside their houses as I passed. My mouth was dry and my face was covered with dust, by the time I got closer to my house. I decided to get down from my donkey and take a drink of water. I splashed water on my face and wiped it dry with my scarf, then I walked slowly toward my house. I saw lights in the house, and they shone outside through a thin curtain. I walked quietly in the dark and felt my heart pound inside my chest.

"What will she do?" I thought, "What will she say?"

I stopped not far from the window and tried to look in. I heard my daughter's voices as they played a game, I heard them laugh, and my heart was happy. I tied my donkey to a post and took a step closer when I saw my wife step in front of the window. I saw her through the curtain, yet she looked down and did not see me, then I saw a man. I stopped and did not move. My eyes were fixed on this man as he walked behind my wife and wrapped his arms around her. I saw her turn and the man leaned down to kiss her.

"Samuel." James said quietly.

I looked up and nodded. I took in a deep breath and sighed.

"Are you able to speak of this?" He asked me.

"I am." I said, and took the last sip of my tea, then put the cup down beside me.

"I returned at night, and when I arrived at my house, I saw my wife through a window."

James leaned forward and listened.

"Then I saw a man put his arms around her and they kissed." I told him.

James sat straight up. "What did you do?"

"I heard my daughters inside playing, and I did not want to disturb them, so I left and went to my parent's house."

"Your wife did not see you?" James asked.

"No, she never did." I answered, "My parents told me that she had divorced me because I did not return, and because I had followed a heretic. The priests were happy that she remarried."

"What did you do?"

"My father told me to leave. He said that Joseph was a good leather smith and had taken over my business at the shop."

"Did you not want to see your children?" James said.

"I wanted nothing more, yet my mother said my children had grieved greatly when I did not return. She told me they were happy now, and that Rachel's new husband was a good father to them. She also believed that I could not come back to live in the same city."

"Who was her new husband?" James asked.

I looked James straight in the eyes, "Thomas."

"What!" James cried out, "The man you left to follow Yeshua with?"

I nodded, "Yes."

"That is why your heart was hurt twice." James acknowledged.

I could only nod, my throat was tight, and I was suddenly tired.

"I understand why you have not spoken of this." James said, "Your story would be criticized by many that do not believe Yeshua was the Messiah, and by those that judge you wrong for leaving your family."

"It took many years to heal my heart, then many years to under-stand, and gain wisdom from what happened." I told him.

"Did you leave that night?" He asked.

"Yes," I said, "I had to go far enough away so people would not recognize me, yet I returned twice each year at night, to visit my parents. They told me about my children yet kept my visits a secret."

"Did you remarry?" James asked.

"No. Rachel was the only woman I loved, and in my heart, she remained my wife." I said.

"When did you travel here?"

"My mother died, and my father not long after, so I believed it was best to leave. My family had their own lives without me."

"I am sorry to hear this Samuel."

"I am at peace James," I said, "I sacrificed much yet I received much also."

"What did you receive?" He asked.

I thought for a moment, I wanted my words to say exactly what I felt.

"I sacrificed all the best of what this world can give you. I sacri-ficed my family, shop and success, yet I received understanding of how God works in our life, my heart grew bigger because God grew in my heart. It is hard to describe those things that I received which are not of this world."

James nodded.

"When I left, I did not know where I was going. I traveled far and stopped along the way to teach and write about Yeshua."

"When did you learn to write?" James asked.

"I learned from the priests when I was a boy." I said.

"What did you write?"

"I wrote what I remembered Yeshua taught, then I would teach those that wanted to know."

"Were you afraid to be called a heretic?" James asked.

"No, I did not stay long in each place, and I did not have followers like Yeshua."

"You are known to be a man of God Samuel. You are respected here."

"Thank you. I appreciate that I was accepted and treated well here. I was able to heal completely in the company of your people."

James reached over and patted my knee. "We are your family now."

I smiled, "Thank you. You are an honorable man."

James stood up, "Will you have some dates?"

I put my hand on the chair and pushed up as I stood. "No, I am tired, I will go home."

"Thank you for telling me your story." James said.

"I was glad to share it with you."

"I will not tell anyone except Deborah, and I will tell her not to speak of it." James said.

"Why do you say this?" I asked.

"I want you to enjoy peace at this time in your life Samuel."

I smiled, "Perhaps waiting until after I pass will be better."

James smiled, "I think it will!"

We said goodnight, and I walked back to my small house. I was glad to have a safe and comfortable place to sleep. Deborah had washed the blankets on my bed this day, then hung them in the sun to dry. When I slipped into bed, it smelled of fresh air and the flowers which are in bloom now. I looked out my window, felt a soft breeze blow in, and closed my eyes. I remembered the color of the flowers that bloomed all around the village.

"Samuel."

I rolled over to look at my door, no one was there. I looked around the room, then closed my eyes again. My legs were stretched out and my arms lay on top of the blanket. I was so comfortable in my bed, that sleep was seeping into my head. I let myself go toward the darkness.

"Samuel."

I heard my name again, yet this time I recognized the voice.

"I am ready." I said, and drifted easily away, to join the one that taught me of unselfish love.

EPILOGUE

*W*hether or not you believe in reincarnation, Jesus, or past life regression therapy, my story is valuable as it gives an example of how important our personal choices are. Personal choices put us on different paths or trajectories that will influence future experiences. Conversely, not making decisions or choices also influence future experiences, the only difference is a person may believe they are not responsible for the outcome. When we take responsibility for our self, we can no longer plead victim to circumstances, and gain wisdom from our bad choices.

The life I lived as a follower of Jesus came with personal sacrifices. I left my family to follow him, not knowing how long I would be gone, or that my decision would have disastrous personal consequences. This is an example of an unconscious renunciation. I made the decision yet was unaware of the results of that decision. This decision was guided by my Higher Self, Spirit Guides, Angels, God or however you label the intelligent co-creator of events in our life. The guidance was felt as a compelling inner urge that could not be denied, an urge that overtook all responsibilities at that time. I called it a Divine Calling, as I was powerless to refuse this inner drive.

This unconscious renunciation served many purposes. Most important being spiritual growth, or experience for the soul, that produces wisdom. I learned that the best of what this world has to offer, such as family, job and success, is not all a human requires to be happy. I learned that without spiritual understanding of who I am, there will always be a void that needs to be filled. Unfortunately, at some point in our evolution, we must give up, or renunciate earthly things in order to receive spiritual gifts. It is a matter of priorities, material or spiritual. There are examples of this all over the planet in many countries.

After countless incarnations, after many varied life experiences, one gains enough self -realization or enlightenment to become a conscious co-creator along with the Divine guidance. This is a generalization, as there are souls that incarnate with full self-realization of who they are, and what their mission is. Although my opinion is that these souls are rare, usually requiring some time to adapt to current life circumstances, before the process of self-realization occurs.

In my current life, I was a conscious co-creator of my renunciation at age thirty-two. It was an excruciating experience over the period of a month, during which I lost twenty pounds from the stress of making my life altering decision. I gave up a wonderful husband and father, home, job, family, and friends to move with my young daughter out of state, so that I might develop spiritually. I was compelled, or received a Divine calling, that required me to leave. I am not advising anyone to do the same, I am only relating my experience. At that time, I did not know this was not only the initiation of renunciation, but also my preincarnation plan, to meet and marry the man that would father my next child.

When I wrote My Life with Jesus, I was already aware that I had a personal connection to him. During my meditations, Jesus came to me on several occasions to deliver messages. Jesus is multidimensional, part of the Christ Consciousness collective, and as such he is able to communicate instantly within the quantum field. Many others have been contacted by Jesus through dreams, visions, meditations, or telepathy, as he is committed to those seeking spiritual guidance.

Although I understood that initiations of renunciation occurred both in my life with Jesus, and in my current life, I didn't fully understand renunciation. I asked Jesus for illumination about this powerful spiritual tool and was awakened at three in the morning with my answer. He came to me telepathically with a download of information that I quickly typed into my smart phone. The following is that channeling from Jesus. I have not altered or edited any sentences or words.

RENUNCIATION INITIATION BY JESUS

APRIL 11, 2020

This initiation is to renounce all worldly reminders of life as cultural, familial and with respect to lineage of incarnations. One must start over in blind faith, not knowing what will come, or how one will survive. Just knowing that love of the Creator, and being a child of the Creator, will allow you to succeed. While being exhilarating, this is also stepping forward into the void, not knowing yet having faith that all will work out as it should.

We would have you remember the pain and agony of making a conscious decision to leave all behind. To give back what the world has given you. This is not to say that you will be without comforts or safety. In this modern incarnation, you would leave one home to reside in another. The test was, do you pick your spiritual life and value your spiritual growth over all else? Cars, houses, family, wealth, prestige, honor, all must come second to your inner desire to know who you are. All great teachers and prophets have gone through this initiation, as well as those that have come as silent prophets upon this earth. Well known teachers and less known members of communities have chosen this path of love over material wealth.

We give you many reasons not to renounce from lovers, partners, established homes, and a happy life, yet what will you decide? What has the largest sway over your decision making? It is not what you have become, but what you will be, so the choice is made by the strongest part of you. Have you evolved to the point when you know who you are, or is there a mysterious part of you demanding that you surrender?

We do not take this lightly. When this initiation is given one must start over, one must begin again, and develop a new persona based on the revelations that manifest from within. This isn't something that is easily explained. Many may mistake this initiation for the dark night of the soul. It is not. This is a turning point in each incarnation that must be addressed and successfully maneuvered. This initiation frees the soul to follow the path which is most rewarding for its spiritual growth.

We ask you to submit to revelations. We ask you to submit to your soul's path, and we ask you to renounce all that is not you. The great renunciation. Love is the ultimate answer to all your questions. Love and soul growth are the ultimate goals of each incarnation, born the difficult way through hard knocks, or through conscious choice. And So It Is.

ABOUT THE AUTHOR

April Autry

April writes about her spiritual journey, including many of her past lives.

April is an intuitive mentor, Quantum healer, Reiki master, yoga teacher, and teaches alignment of your mind-body-soul through consciousness expansion and spiritual practices.

Books, meditations, courses and spiritual lifestyle products can be found on her website:

GalacticGrandmother.com

April enjoys reading your book reviews, so please feel free to email her at:

info@galacticgrandmother.com

www.ingramcontent.com/pod-product-compliance
Lightning Source LLC
LaVergne TN
LVHW051430080426
835508LV00022B/3333